RENT-A-MAID
INTERNATIONAL

Rent-A-Maid International

An American Dream Instruction Manual

Raymond H. Kiker, Sr.

To order additional copies of this book, contact:
Xlibris Corporation
1-888-795-4274
www.Xlibris.com
Orders@Xlibris.com
92454

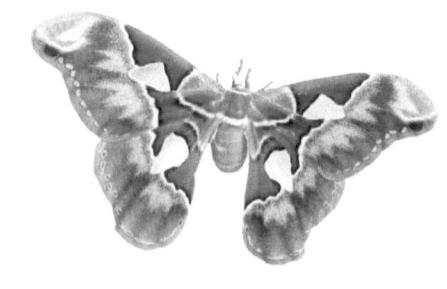

Good Morning!

THIS BOOK WAS WRITTEN IN FAITH. IN HOPES THAT AS YOU READ, YOUR FAITH WILL INCREASE. READ ON!

ACKNOWLEDGMENT

The most influential people in my life were my Grandfather and Grandmother. They somehow instilled in me "Good Values", Honesty, and integrity. Next, where people like W. Clement Stone, Napoleon Hill, Dolly Parton, Merle Haggard, George Jones, Vince Gill, Mike McClain, President George Bush and Laura, and finely Happy Delsigne for her endless efforts to dot the I's and cross the T's.

I learned to live by two simple rules: "Do the right thing, because it's the right thing to do". And, "Do it now"!

Happiness, Freedom and Peace
of mind, are always attained
by giving them to someone else!

Corporations Section
P.O.Box 13697
Austin, Texas 78711-3697

Phil Wilson
Secretary of State

Office of the Secretary of State

CERTIFICATE OF FILING
OF

RENT-A-MAID INTERNATIONAL LLC
File Number: 800977421

The undersigned, as Secretary of State of Texas, hereby certifies that a Certificate of Formation for the above named Domestic Limited Liability Company (LLC) has been received in this office and has been found to conform to the applicable provisions of law.

ACCORDINGLY, the undersigned, as Secretary of State, and by virtue of the authority vested in the secretary by law, hereby issues this certificate evidencing filing effective on the date shown below.

The issuance of this certificate does not authorize the use of a name in this state in violation of the rights of another under the federal Trademark Act of 1946, the Texas trademark law, the Assumed Business or Professional Name Act, or the common law.

Dated: 05/12/2008

Effective: 05/12/2008

Phil Wilson
Secretary of State

Come visit us on the internet at http://www.sos.state.tx.us/

Phone: (512) 463-5555
Prepared by: Virginia Tobias

Fax: (512) 463-5709
TID: 10306

Dial: 7-1-1 for Relay Services
Document: 215233210002

11

TABLE OF CONTENTS

"RENT-A-MAID"

First and most important I want to say thank you. You have taken an important initial step towards a goal or idea you have hoped for. Don't slow down or think of stopping, don't let other things interrupt or sidestep your thoughts. Find a quiet place by yourself and study the materials we have sent you.

The material that is in the manuscript "How to Operate a Rent-A-Maid Business" is everything you will need to know, and to try to absorb all of the information in one reading would be impossible. Have an extra sheet of paper to write down your questions and thoughts as you read. It has taken fifteen years to acquire the information you have and it should take several readings to get the over-all view.

If you still have questions that you feel are unanswered, please call. We're here to help.

Thanks again,
Ray Kiker
1-972-240-4098

ENCOURAGEMENT

FAVOR IS DECEITFUL AND BEAUTY IS VAIN BUT A WOMAN THAT FEARS THE LORD, SHE SHALL BE PRAISED.

DREAM YOUR DREAMS. REALIZE THAT THE FIRST STEP TOWARDS MAKING DREAMS COME TRUE IS TO WAKE UP, GET UP AND PLAN. THE HEIGHTS OF TOMORROW ARE WAITING FOR THE YOUNG MEN AND WOMEN WHO HAVE THE FAITH, THE COURAGE AND THE FRIENDSHIP TO START CLIMBING TOWARDS THEM TODAY.

REMEMBER, SUCCESS IS JUST ANOTHER NAME FOR YOUR UNLIMITED POWER TO BE MORE CREATIVE, UNDERSTANDING, COURAGEOUS, HUMBLE, HELPFUL, DARING, DETERMINED AND DYNAMIC. GENUINE SUCCESS HAS NO RELATIONSHIP TO WHAT YOU ARE NOW. IT IS IN YOUR POWER TO BE THE PERSON YOU CAN BECOME.

A JOURNEY OF A THOUSAND MILES BEGINS WITH THE FIRST STEP.

IT IS NOT IN LIFE'S CHANCES BUT IN ITS CHOICES THAT HAPPINESS COMES TO THE HEART OF THE INDIVIDUAL.

CAST NOT AWAY, THEREFORE YOUR CONFIDENCE, WHICH HATH GREAT RECOMPENSE OF REWARD.
HEBREWS 10:35

TIME AND OPPORTUNITY COME TO EVERYONE.

TROUBLES ARE OFTEN THE TOOLS BY WHICH GOD FASHIONS US FOR BETTER THINGS.

FOR WHERE YOUR TREASURE IS, THERE WILL YOUR HEART BE ALSO.

HOW "RENT-A-MAID" BEGAN

Hello, my name is "Sharon (Kiker) Hammond". I opened 'RENT-A-MAID" of Oklahoma City, Ok in March 1983. It was a real challenge! I found a nice office, put in a phone and printed business cards. I was off to a flying start!!!

But I had no one to do the cleaning and no one knew I was open!!!

My husband, Ray and I were die hards. We began making signs in our garage and putting them out in the nicer areas of town. We had never run a maid service before and we would have starved except for our existing business of selling baby furniture.

We finally started getting busy and things came to us as we needed them: a theft bond for our maids, a general cleaning check list, a check list for vacant houses and apartment cleaning, even iron-ons for T-shirts., yellow page ads, newspaper ads and most of all , the "Pricelist for Cleaning." Just imagine, we cleaned our first apartment for $5.00, it was 4 rooms. We kept that price for six months and when we decided to go up a dollar we actually had people quit! Most of them came back later.

Thanks for listening, you're in good hands with my "X" Ray Kiker. He's a fair and Godly man, and this is my story of how Rent-A-Maid began.

Sharon E. Hammond
Sharon Hammond

"Faith comes by hearing and hearing by the word of God"

RENT-A-MAID
INTERNATIONAL

Thank you . . . Muchas gracias . . . Tusen tak . . . Merci beaucoup. No matter what language you speak you can own and operate a Rent-A-Maid business. The boundaries of how large or how many areas in which you operate are only in your dreams.

WHAT YOU THINK YOU BECOME

Always think positive thoughts; your thoughts control you right down to your next step. Never give up. Take a vacation yes, but remember you need to get back up some day. The sooner the better: get started and get back to work.

It may sound like I am writing this to myself, and I am. I closed my Rent-A-Maid office in Oklahoma City in the fall of 1997. I enjoyed running Rent-A-Maid; it was fun, exciting, challenging and sometimes it was a heartbreaking job, but it was easy.

So, ten years later, I'm starting again.

I'm a strong believer in God, the Holy Spirit and Jesus. I believe that those who believe in him succeed in ways that the secular world would not believe. If you are a believer, that was the biggest step that you have ever made. No one is perfect, but we can strive in that direction.

Your next big step is to make up your mind that you're going to do this. As Napoleon Hill once said,

"Do it now"

BEFORE OPENING YOUR OFFICE

I've made a list of things you will need to do before officially opening your Rent-A-Maid office: Basic things such as going to the courthouse and listing your company name (DBA: Doing Business As), registering your name as owner of the business, so that this is on file where you will be operating as a legitimate business. The cost to do this is generally $10-$20.

Oh yes, don't forget to call us and let us know that you have decided to open a Rent-A-Maid office and reserve your special ZIP code(s). Only one person can operate as Rent-A-Maid in a ZIP code designated area. Read our contracts for details on benefits like system instruction, daily guidance and the benefits of being with a company that cares that you succeed. And I do care.

After you have registered your name with the courthouse, your next stop would be the bank. Unless they know you at the bank, you will probably need the paperwork you received from the courthouse to open a business checking account. Select a bank that you have done business with, if possible.

After you have ordered and received your business cards, give everyone in the bank your card. Hand out your business card to everyone you see during the day; at the grocery store, gas station and hardware store. When you go shopping give the sales clerks a card. Working people may not have the time to do their own housecleaning and are potential customers. Tell them to call the office for pricing. Your time is valuable, so don't spend too much time visiting. Spend just enough time to create the desire for the service.

YOUR HOME OFFICE

An extra bedroom in your home is a perfect location for your Home Office which would be eligible for a tax deduction. Items used in your business such as furniture, art, and office supplies, printing costs, licensing, dues and a portion of your home utilities are deductible. Your accountant can further advise you in this area.

BE INEXPENSIVE

"Be inexpensive but not cheap. Cheap gets you nowhere; Inexpensive saves you money." I once shared an office with a tanning salon. We answered their phones on their lunch hour and they returned the favor when we were out of the office.

BUSINESS PHONE

A business phone is important. Generally, the phone company will give you a free Yellow Page listing. You should also have a listing under "Maid Service" as well as "Housecleaning". Tip: use BOLD letters for the listing.

You should try to acquire a number that is easy to remember, such as 6243 as those digits spell "maid". I purchased 6243 from an individual in order to get that specific number. The number doesn't have to be in the area you are in; the telephone company can put a Call forward on the number.

Most of your daily responsibilities can be finished by noon, if you start at 8 AM you should be able to close by 2 PM. Schedules for the following day can be given out before leaving the office.

"Confirm All Schedules for the Following Day"

When you first open your office you will need to advertise; possibly distributing your business cards to apartment managers, etc. I'm a big believer in free-standing signs posted on poles once or twice in an area which can generate business for up to six months. Advertise where your business takes you. When a home is cleaned in an area, make sure business cards are left at the homes on either side and across the street from that appointment. Having a presence in most of the good areas of town can help your business grow at a fast pace. The name recognition of "Rent-A-Maid" will help tremendously. Small classified ads can be placed in the daily newspaper, community Green Sheet and Craig's list.

PRICING

The first cleaning of a home or a vacant apartment cleaning should be charged by the hour. After the first cleaning a set price can be established according to the number of rooms to be cleaned, using our General Cleaning Checklist. Be sure which rooms are to be cleaned because customers often do not have their entire home cleaned.

USING YOUR SUPPLIES OR THE CUSTOMER'S

Most customers will have some cleaning supplies and/or a good vacuum cleaner, however, it is easier to bring your own supplies and charge accordingly.

WHAT WE DO FOR YOU

This instruction manual will be updated continually as things change, keeping fresh ideas at your fingertips.

1. We will assign you an exclusive area either through a number of assigned ZIP codes, area boundaries or cities.
2. We will print checklists, business cards, scheduling cards, signs, area manager pamphlets, training letter, etc. as part of your start up package.
3. We will list your name on our website.
4. Our Help Line (972-240-4098) is available to you for questions.

INTERVIEWS AND TRAINING

A small ad in the Help Wanted section of the Sunday paper usually draws enough calls to hire the maids you will need. Also consider using the newspapers online postings, as well as local metropolitan Craig's List. Divide your areas into ZIP codes with approximately 100,000 people in each area.

It makes no difference if your new maids are short, tall, slim or large. Ethnic background isn't a factor either. You will find good workers in all sizes, shapes and ethnicity. I once interviewed a woman who weighed nearly 300 pounds. I didn't hire her right away because I feared she would break items in the homes. She became my best maid! Many customers asked for her personally and she never broke a thing!

Speaking of breakage, I estimate that I have paid less than $300 for breakage. I dealt with the customer and arrived at a fair price for the broken item and the maid and I split the cost. Caution your maids to let you know if something was broken and handle it right away. Call the customer and get it settled. Unsettled breakage problems may affect your maid's performance.

Interviews are usually held on Monday and Tuesday. Calls coming from the "help wanted" ads have usually stopped by Wednesday. A two-day school for your new maids can be held the following Monday before they are sent out to clean. They are out making money by Wednesday!!

Applicants should bring a notebook and pen for training notes. Training should start by 9 AM to be finished by Noon. You could serve coffee and have snacks available. Training should be kept light, upbeat and positive. Go through each checklist and explain how to get their next day's schedule

Interviews and Training

And what supplies to carry with them. At the end of the first day's training give each person a General Cleaning Checklist and encourage them to go home and clean their own home or apartment with this list.

On their second day of training you can discuss taxes and assigning areas. I usually let the maids choose the zip code areas that are open. Middle class areas are best, high income areas generally have full-time maids.

After their areas have been selected the advertising begins! Allow for 1 to 2 hours daily for the maids to advertise in their area by putting out signs and business cards. Working in pairs can be productive and fun!!

Maids must have a car and mobile phone and dress appropriately. T-shirts and pants/slacks are an appropriate suggestion.

The maid's kit consists of the Vacant House Checklist, General Cleaning Checklist, business cards and signs to post in their area. They will also need notebooks to record customer cleaning instructions, directions to the home, where the key will be for home access, cat/dog's name, etc. We are in the service business, so spoil the customer. Some business managers send "Thank You" cards after the first cleaning appointment.

****A SUCCESSFUL OFFICE HIRES AND SETS APPOINTMENTS AT THE SAME TIME***

People move, visit relatives, has special parties. Holidays are our busiest times. A family from New York visiting relatives in Dallas can be assured that if they were treated right by Rent-A-Maid in New York, they can certainly recommend Rent-A-Maid in Dallas. Our checklists are the same. Our maids move or change locations and can transfer very easily, working with Rent-A-Maid in California, or Florida, maybe even Europe! Bonuses and training are the same throughout Rent-A-Maid.

ESSENTIALS FOR A HEALTHY LIFESTYLE!

Develop a Relationship with God! As your relationship grows, you will enjoy all the blessings God has to offer!

Develop Acceptance! Practicing acceptance clears your mind of needless anxiety, freeing you to enjoy life!

Practice Gratitude! Gratitude brings instant joy, builds you body's physical defenses, and reduces stress!

Be forgiving! As you let go of negative feelings toward others, you will find greater peace and optimism!

Give and receive love! Heart-focused, sincere, and positive feelings boost the immune system!

Enjoy Activity! An active lifestyle enables every system in your body to work better!

Eat Nutritiously! Choosing healthy, whole foods minimizes blood sugar swings!

Sleep Peacefully! Establishing a bedtime routine will help you sleep longer and more soundly!

Drink Water! Proper hydration is essential for every organ and system in your body!

Breathe Deeply! Deep breathing releases body toxins faster than any other means!

There is one other way to live a happy life style, and that is to have enough money to pay your bills. So let's get going, remember, "Exercise daily, walk with God".

Scheduling Board & Cards

The scheduling board can be any board large enough to make six 8" squares for each day of the week, excluding Sunday. Leave room on the left side for the maid's name.

The scheduling cards should have the following information about the customer when you set an appointment.

NAME:
ADDRESS:
TOWN, ZIP:
HOME PHONE:
OFFICE PHONE:
ACCESS INTO HOUSE:
DIRECTIONS:
NUMBER OF ROOMS TO CLEAN:
DATE TO CLEAN:
HOW OFTEN:
AMOUNT $

	Monday	Tuesday	Wednesday	Thursday	Friday	Saturday
Maids Name!						

This is for one maids schedule, make as many as you have Maids.

SCHEDULING

Scheduling is as easy as 1, 2, 3, if you have a plan. (Refer to the drawing of the scheduling board). There's probably a computer program for scheduling, but a lot can happen when your computer goes crazy. Sometimes the old way is best.

I use a bulletin board for scheduling; stick pins are easy to hold the scheduling cards on the board. The important thing is to get all the information about the customer; when to clean, how to get in, where the supplies are, and the number of rooms to clean and the cash or check amount.

"Hi, this is Rent-A-Maid, my name is _____. We're scheduled to clean your house tomorrow at ___am. OK? I understand we are to clean ____ rooms? The key is located _____ and the supplies are located _____ and the check or cash for $_____ will be on the kitchen table. Is this all correct?

This information is to be given to the Maid who will do the cleaning.

Every Friday your scheduling board should be set up for the following week. The cards are turned horizontal for that week's work. Cards turned vertical are for the following week or monthly cleaning. Some people schedule their cleaning far in advance. Always confirm the next day work schedule. When you confirm the schedule, put a small note with the stick pin that says "confirmed" or "w/c" for you to call back if you can't confirm with the client.

This simple method tells you how many Maids are working, how many houses are being cleaned, and the areas. This will help you decide if you should hire more maids and/or advertise in an area?

Wednesday's or Thursday's are good days for the Maids to bring the checks to the office for that weeks cleaning. They should pick up more checklists, signs, and business cards, and have a short meeting to express how important it is to advertise. Weekends are a good time to put out signs and cards. Pay checks are mailed the following week.

Note: Remember, character is reflected in to each one of the Maids by your actions, how you speak, dress, act, and how the office looks. When problems arise, oh yes, they do happen, and when they do happen, remember problems are a way to grow. So if you have a problem, that's good. It will only take you in another direction.

"Fear knocked at your hearts door. Faith answered, and nobody was there".

You've heard, "Get her done," "Go to it girl," laugh, nothing last forever. What doesn't kill you makes you stronger. Right!

Be more than just an office person. Made sure you girls have gas money, the right cleaning supplies, clean hair and clothes, and that they are in the right frame of mind. Some offices put pick-me-up pamphlets in with their paychecks. Read a good positive book yourself. The 'Holy Bible" is a good place to start. Believe it or not, in my daily reading, the Bible has actually talked about the same problems I've had that day. It's unreal.

The Army has a good saying, "Be all you can be". "Its not where you're standing right now, it's what direction you are moving".

Live so that when your girls think of fairness, caring, integrity, they think of you.

Things are possible, until they're not.

Last: Things don't go wrong and break your heart so you can become bitter and give up. They happen to break you down and build you up so you can be all that you were intended to be.

Note you might want to put one of these in with the paychecks.

TRUTHS!

One of the best ways to persuade others is with your ears, listen to them.

When character is lost, all is lost.

A poor person is not a person without a cent but a person who is without a dream.

A great leader's courage to fulfill their vision comes from passion, not position.

"When you're down to nothing God is up to something. Worry looks around, Sorry looks back and Faith looks up."

Love is life . . . if you miss love, you miss life. Being deeply loved by someone gives you strength while loving someone deeply gives you courage.

The best portion of a woman's life is her little nameless, unremembered acts of kindness and love.

The difference between impossible and possible lies in a person's determination.

The person who says it cannot be done should not interrupt the person that is doing it.

Be determined to handle any challenge in a way that will make you grow.

Writing causes thinking.

Discipline is the bridge between goals and accomplishments.

Happiness, Freedom and Peace of Mind are always attained by giving them to someone else.

Right attitudes produce right actions. DO THE RIGHT THING BECAUSE IT IS THE RIGHT THING TO DO!!

CAVEMEN NEED RENT-A-MAID

Many years ago during the caveman era Rent-a-Maid was started. Oh yes, the caveman needed someone to clean out the animal droppings, bones left from their killing wild animals, and of course, all the mess they make partying after a big hunt!

No doubt some inspired cavewoman thought, "These cavemen need help" in keeping their spears, bows and arrows and loin skins where they could find them in case a large mammal came calling, much less another cavewoman. So . . .

Rent-a-Cavewoman was born!

Today, we've only changed the name to bring it up to speed, so to speak. So get out there and clean some caves, houses or apartments. Make some caveman, oh I mean some 'hunk' a little more pleasant to be with when he brings his favorite girl home for the evening or for the rest of his life. Know what I mean?

Remember, stick a business card behind the door below the sink!

EIGHT WAYS TO INCREASE YOUR FAITH

1. *Faith by Hearing: Romans 10:17 So then faith cometh by hearing and hearing by the Word of God.*
2. *Faith Seeks God: Hebrews 11:6 But without faith it is impossible to please him, for he that cometh to God must believe that he is and that he is a rewarder of them that diligently seek him.*
3. *Faith acts: James 2:17 Even so faith, if it hath not works is dead, being alone.*
4. *Faith Speaks : 2 Corinthians 4:13 We having the same spirit of faith . . . . I believed, and therefore have I spoken; we also believed, and therefore speak;*
5. *Faith Worketh By Love: Galatians 5:14 For all the law is fulfilled in one word, even in this; thou shalt love thy neighbor as thyself.*
6. *Faith Works in Hope: Hebrews 11:1 Now faith is the substance of things hoped for, the evidence of things not seen.*
7. *Faith works With Patience: Hebrews 6:12 That ye be not slothful, but followers of them who through faith and patience inherit the promises.*
8. *Faith Gives God Thanks: Colossians 2:7 Rooted, built up in him and established in the faith as you have been taught, abounding therein with THANKSGIVING.*

BE DETERMINED

"Be determined to handle any challenge I don't care how much power, brilliance, or energy you have, if you don't harness it and focus it on a specific target, and hold it there, you're never going to accomplish as much as your ability warrants". Zig Zigler

"Joy is the feeling of grinning inside". Melba Colgrove

"If I wanted to become a tramp, I would seek information and advice from the most successful tramp I could find. If I wanted to become a failure, I would seek advice from people who have never succeeded. If I wanted to succeed in all things, I would look around me for those who are succeeding, and do as they have done". Joseph Marshall Wade

"Continuous effort—not strength or intelligence—is the key to unlocking our potential". Sir Winston Churchill

Procrastination is the natural assassin of opportunity.

"Strength does not come from winning. Your struggles develop your strengths. When you go through hardships and decide not to surrender, that is strength." Arnold Schwarzenegger

"Nothing limits achievement like small thinking; nothing expands possibilities like unleashed imagination. Adversity causes some men to break; others to break records. The person who removes a mountain begins by carrying away small stones. Greatness is not found in possessions, power, position, or prestige.

It is discovered in goodness, humility, service, and character. When you paint success pictures in your mind, you initiate an inner process whereby your attitudes, hopes, aspirations, and enthusiasm are elevated in response to an image of a more promising future. Every person who aspires must first sell themselves hope, the promise of a better life. It is wise to direct your anger towards problems—not people; Focus your energies on answers—not excuses". William Arthur Ward

KAYLEE NICOLE KIKER, MY GRANDDAUGHTER

Faith, Hope and Love, but the greatest of these is

LOVE!

LACK OF MONEY

"Lack of money is no obstacle. Lack of an idea is an obstacle". Ken Hakuta

"The gem cannot be polished without friction". Chinese proverb

"Ride on! Rough-shod if need be, smooth-shod if that will do, but ride on! Ride over all obstacles, and win the race"! Charles Dickens

"Act as if what you do makes a difference. It does". William James

"In order to do what really matters to you. First, know what really matters to you". Dr. Edward Hallowell

"You can't help someone get up a hill without getting closer to the top yourself". H. Norman Schwarzkopf

"The majority of men meet with failure because of their lack of persistence in creating new plans to take the place of those, which fail". Napoleon Hill

"Belief always precedes action". James Allen

"A warrior doesn't give up what he loves . . . he finds the love in what he does". Socrates

"A life lived with integrity—even if it lacks the trappings of fame and fortune is a shining star in whose light others may follow in the years to come". Denis Waitley

Believe while others are doubting. Plan while others are playing.

Study while others are sleeping. Decide while others are delaying.

Prepare while others are daydreaming. Begin while others are procrastinating. Work while others are wishing. Save while others are wasting. Listen while others are talking. Smile while others are frowning. Commend while others are criticizing. Persist while others are quitting.

"The price of excellence is discipline. The cost of mediocrity is disappointment". William Arthur Ward

"Kindness is the language which the deaf can hear and the blind can see". Mark Twain

WHEN YOU WORK FOR RENT-A-MAID !

"BE CHEERFUL AND TAKE PRIDE IN YOUR WORK"

You must be willing to work hard and full time. You are expected to be on the job on time. You must have a dependable car. You do not smoke in a client's home. DO NOT ANSWER OR USE THE CLIENT'S TELEPHONE. Do not discuss your personal life with the client. The best policy is to work and do little talking. You must furnish your own lunch.

Remember, your time is your own, the sooner you finish a house the more time you have for another assignment. The more houses you clean, the more money you make.

NO JOB IS DEMEANING, only YOU can make it so by your actions or poor work quality.

YOUR APPEARANCE IS IMPORTANT. Your hair and clothing should be clean, neat and appropriate. R.A.M. T-SHIRTS when available.

THE TIME OF YOUR APPOINTMENTS is made for the convenience and at the request of the client. A 9 AM appointment means being on the job at 9 AM, not leaving home at that time. Go to your appointments in sequence, not second first, etc. If you are not able to make an appointment on time, call the office ASAP and the client will be notified. If you cannot keep an appointment, call the office and arrangements will be made. If you get lost, run out of gas or have car trouble, call the office for help. We will set your appointment addresses as close together as possible, but you will be expected to be at your appointments, on time, wherever they are. BEING LATE OR FAILING TO KEEP AN APPOINTMENT IS A VALID COMPLAINT.

SECURITY. Call as soon as you get to the job so we will know you are there. Call when you are leaving and we will give you your next appointment. This is for your security and protection.

CIRCUMSTANCES

"People are anxious to improve their circumstances, but are unwilling to improve themselves. They therefore remain bound". James Allen

Blessed are those that can give without remembering and receive without forgetting.

"Let us be grateful to people who make us happy; they are the charming gardeners who make our souls blossom". Marcel Proust

"I feel a very unusual sensation—if it is not indigestion,

I think it must be gratitude". Benjamin Disraeli

"One's philosophy is not best expressed in words. It is expressed in the choices one makes. In the long run, we shape our lives and we shape ourselves.

The process never ends until we die. And, the choices we make are ultimately our own responsibility". Eleanor Roosevelt

"Doubt, of whatever kind, can be ended by action alone". Thomas Carlyle

"It is not the strongest of the species that survive, nor the most intelligent, but the one most responsive to change". Charles Darwin

"Dreams are renewable. No matter what our age or condition, there are still untapped possibilities within us and new beauty waiting to be born". Dale Turner

(Dream big dreams, then put on your overalls and go out and make the dreams come true.)

"My basic principle is that you don't make decisions because they are easy; You don't make them because they are cheap; You don't make them because they're popular; You make them because they're right". Theodore Hesburgh

"If human beings are perceived as potentials rather than problems, as possessing strengths instead of weaknesses, as unlimited rather that dull and unresponsive, then they thrive and grow to their capabilities". Barbara Bush

When you arrive on the job; count the rooms, find the supplies, and the check. Call the office if the number of rooms does not correspond with your instructions or the check is not there and/or for the wrong amount, or you cannot find the supplies. If the client is home and the rooms do not correspond, call the office and we will talk to them. We do not refuse to do anything reasonable (such as carrying the vacuum cleaner upstairs or sweeping stairs).

The checklist is to be followed unless otherwise instructed by the client. Sloppy or incomplete work loses clients. Sometimes the house will look clean to you but a client that is particular will notice if something has not been touched. The house should shine when you are through!!

THREE OR MORE VALID COMPLAINTS IN ONE WEEK IS GROUNDS FOR DISMISSAL. Our work is guaranteed. A valid complaint requires you to return and redo the work without pay.

YOU ARE A BUSINESS PERSON REPRESENTING RENT-A-MAID, BE AN OUTSTANDING REPRESENTATIVE!!

"There is one **CHRISTMAS CAROL** that has always baffled me. What in the world do leaping lords, French hens, swimming swans, and especially the partridge who won't come out of the pear tree, have to do with Christmas? This week, I found out. From 1558 until 1829, Roman Catholics in England were not permitted to practice their faith openly. Someone, during that era, wrote this carol as a catechism song for young Catholics. It was written with two levels of meaning: the surface meaning & a hidden deeper meaning known only to members of their church. Each element in the carol has a code word for reality which the children could remember.-The partridge in a pear tree was Jesus Christ.-Two turtle doves were the Bible's Old and New Testaments.-Three French hens stood for faith, hope and love.—The four calling birds were the four gospels of Matthew, Mark, Luke & John. The five golden rings recalled the Torah or Law, the first five books of the Old Testament.—The six geese a-laying stood for the Six Days of Creation.—Seven swans a-swimming represented the sevenfold gifts of the Holy Spirit-Prophesy, Serving, Teaching, Exhortation, Contribution, Leadership & Mercy.—The eight maids a-milking were the eight Beatitudes.—Nine ladies dancing were the nine Fruits of the Holy Spirit-Love, Joy, Peace, Patience, Kindness, Goodness,

Faithfulness, Gentleness, and Self Control.—The ten lords a-leaping were The Ten Commandments.—The eleven pipers piping stood for the eleven faithful Disciples.—The twelve drummers drumming symbolized the twelve points of belief in the Apostles' Creed.

"There are no limitations to the mind except those we acknowledge; both poverty and riches are the offspring of thought". Napoleon Hill

"Most people never run far enough on their first wind to find out if they've got a second. Give your dreams all you've got and you'll be amazed at the energy that comes out of you". William James

"He who would learn to fly one day must first learn to stand and walk and run and climb and dance; one cannot fly into flying". Friedrich Nietzsche(1844-1900, German Philosopher)

"You can conquer almost any fear if you will make up your mind to do so. For remember, fear doesn't exist anywhere except in the mind". Dale Carnegie". Change the changeable, accept the unchangeable, and remove yourself from the unacceptable". Denis Waitley

"Associate yourself with men of good quality, if you esteem your own reputation; for it is better to be alone than in bad company". George Washington

"Joy is what happens when we allow ourselves to recognize how good things really are". Marianne Williamson

"Life is a romantic business, but you have to make the romance. Oliver Wendell Holmes

ANSWERING THE PHONE!

Rent-A-maid, this is _____. *Are you calling for a one time cleaning, or a regular cleaning?*

WEEKLY OR EVERY TWO WEEK CLEANING!

We have a general cleaning check-list we use to clean your home. Our maids are bonded for theft, and we use your cleaning supplies or ours with additional charge. Our first cleaning is by the hour. We charge $_____ per hour (three hour minimum). We are a member of the Better Business Bureau, and we guarantee our service. After your first cleaning, we charge by the number of rooms you want cleaned. Count the number of rooms you want cleaned, bathrooms count as a room, and I can give you an estimate. _____ (five room's minimum). If you are not home, let us know where the key is to get in, and leave a check on the kitchen table payable to Rent-A-maid. We will call the day before to remind you that we are scheduled to clean the next day. You can change the rooms to be cleaned, if you have company coming or a special event this will help.

VACANT HOUSE OR APARTMENT CLEANING! We have a Vacant House or Apartment check list. If you want extra cleaning, such as inside the oven and refrigerator, walls, windows, etc. "Read extra cleaning list". We charge $_____ per hour, (Three hour minimum). There is an extra charge of $_____ if we bring our supplies. Our maids are bonded for theft, and we guarantee our service. How soon would you like your place cleaned?

SMILE, your attitude is contagious: always has a positive attitude!

LOVE!

"Love is like playing the piano. First you must learn to play by the rules, then you must forget the rules and play from your heart.

The thought manifests as the word. The word manifests as the deed.

The deed develops into habit. And the habit hardens into character.

So watch the thought and its ways with care. And let it spring from love, born out of concern for all beings". Buddha

What makes a weak man brave. And a king step off his throne. Good times, bad times. Easy times, tough times, it comes in an instant. And lasts three days after forever, that's what love is. Buddha

"The hardest arithmetic to master is that which enables us to count our blessings". Eric Hoffer

"The strongest single factor in prosperity consciousness is self-esteem: believing you can do it, believing you deserve it, believing you will get it". Jerry Gillies

"No stream or gas drives anything until it is confined. No Niagara is ever turned into light and power until it is tunneled. No life ever grows great until it is focused, dedicated and disciplined". Harry E. Fosdick

"Life is like riding a bike. It is impossible to maintain your balance while standing still". Linda Brakeall

"It doesn't matter which side of the fence you get off on sometimes.

What matters most is getting off. You cannot make progress without making decisions". Jim Rohn

"The first step toward change is acceptance. Once you accept yourself, you open the door to change. That's all you have to do. Change is not something you do, it's something you allow". Will Garcia

"Judge each day not by the harvest you reap but by the seeds you plant". Robert Louis Stevenson

"Perhaps the most valuable result of all education is the ability to make yourself do the thing you have to do, when it ought to be done, whether you like it or not". Thomas Huxley

Vacant House/Apartment Checklist

Customers name _____

Address _____

Your personal Maid _____ Date _____

LIVING ROOM AND FAMILY ROOM: check for cobwebs. Clean mirrors and patio doors. Clean inside closets and shelves. Clean windowsills and baseboards. Vacuum last.

KITCHEN: clean countertops, stovetop, refrigerator, clean inside cabinets and under sink. Clean window sills and baseboards. Scour sink last and shine chrome. Mop floor (wax if needed).

BATHROOMS: scrub bathtub or shower, walls and floor. Scrub toilet and sink, inside outside and around base of toilet. Clean countertops, mirrors, and windowsills. Shine all faucets. Mop floor (wax if needed).

BEDROOMS: check for cobwebs. Clean mirrors. Dust windowsills and baseboards. Clean inside closets and shelves. Vacuum last.

CARPORT OR GARAGE: sweep and clean storage shed and shelves. Empty all trash in trashcans. Check patio and walkways for trash.

If for any reason you are not satisfied, please call our local office immediately. Thank you for your business. "RENT-A-MAID".

An Angel says, 'Never borrow from the future. If you worry about what may happen tomorrow and it doesn't happen, you have worried in vain. Even if it does happen, you have to worry twice.'

1. Pray
2. Go to bed on time.
3. Get up on time so you can start the day unrushed.
4. Say No to projects that won't fit into your time schedule, or that will compromise your mental health.
5. Delegate tasks to capable others.
6. Simplify and unclutter your life.
7. Less is more. (Although one is often not enough, two are often too many.)
8. Allow extra time to do things and to get to places.
9. Pace yourself. Spread out big changes and difficult projects over time; don't lump the hard things all together.
10. Take one day at a time.
11. Separate worries from concerns. If a situation is a concern, find out what God would have you do and let go of the anxiety. If you can't do anything about a situation, forget it.
12. Live within your budget; don't use credit cards for ordinary purchases.
13. Have backups; an extra car key in your wallet, an extra house key buried in the garden, extra stamps, etc.
14. K.M.S. (Keep Mouth Shut). This single piece of advice can prevent an enormous amount of trouble.
15. Do something for the Kid in You every day.
16. Carry a Bible with you to read while waiting in line.
17. Get enough rest.
18. Eat right.
19. Get organized so everything has its place.
20. Listen to a tape while driving that can help improve your quality of life.
21. Write down thoughts and inspirations.
22. Every day, find time to be alone.

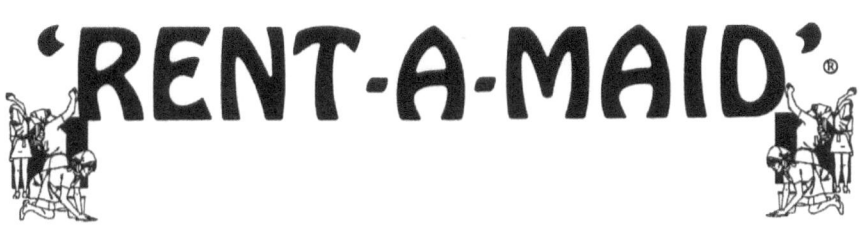

CUSTOMER'S NAME _____

ADDRESS _____

YOUR PERSONAL MAID _____ DATE _____

BEDROOMS:

_____ Check for cobwebs

_____ Straighten room pick up toys, hang up clothes

_____ Dust: window sills, headboard & footboard on bed, dresser & end tables, dust under everything (use polish or wax)

_____ Clean mirrors

_____ Take out trash and empty & wash ash trays

_____ Make beds: (change sheets if clean sheets are left out)

_____ Vacuum: move end tables and chairs, clean in corners, sweep under bed

BATHROOMS:

_____ Take out trash

_____ Scrub bathtub or shower: walls and floor

_____ Scrub toilet and sink: inside, outside, and around base of toilet

_____ Clean countertops, mirrors, and window sills

_____ Mop floor (wax if needed)

_____ Shine all faucets

KITCHEN:

_____ Take out trash

_____ Wash dishes and all ash trays

_____ Clean countertops, stovetop, kitchen table, refrigerator (dust top of refrigerator), clean under everything on table and cabinets

_____ Dust window sills, legs and crossboards of table and chairs

_____ Mop floor (wax if needed)

_____ Scour sink last, and shine chrome

LIVING ROOM AND/OR FAMILY ROOM:

_____ Check for cobwebs

_____ Straighten room pick up everything

_____ Clean mirrors and patio doors

_____ Dust: window sills, picture frames, under everything on shelves and tables, legs and crossboards on tables and TV

_____ Vacuum: move end tables, coffee tables, chairs, footstools, and anything reasonable; shake throw rugs outside and pick up anything on carpet that vacuum didn't get

If for any reason you are not satisfied, please call our local office immediately.

Thank you for your business,

RAY KIKER, President
_____

49

PROBLEMS!

23. Having problems? Talk to God on the spot. Try to nip small problems in the bud. Don't wait until it's time to go to bed to try and pray.

24. Make friends with Godly people

25. Keep a folder of favorite scriptures on hand.

26. Remember that the shortest bridge between despair and hope is often a good 'Thank you Jesus!

27. Laugh.

28. Laugh some more!

29. Take your work seriously, but not yourself at all.

30. Develop a forgiving attitude (most people are doing the best they c31. Be kind to unkind people (they probably need it the most).

32. Sit on your ego.

33. Talk less; listen more.

34. Slow down.

35. Remind yourself that you are not the general manager of the universe.

36. Every night before bed, think of one thing you're grateful for that you've never been grateful for before. GOD HAS A WAY OF TURNING THINGS AROUND FOR YOU.

'If God is for us! Who can be against us?'

"Being defeated is only a temporary condition;

Giving up is what makes it permanent". Marilyn vos Savant

"Out of difficulties grow miracles". Jean De La Bruyere

"The question isn't who is going to let me; It's who is going to stop me". Ayn Rand

"Many things which cannot be overcome when they are together yield themselves up when taken little by little". Plutarch

Be sure to get the check,
fill out the check-list and leave it on
the kitchen table or countertop!

Knocking on Heaven's Door!

Knock, Knock I knocked at heaven's door this morning. God asked me . . . 'My child, what can I do for you?' And I said, 'Father, please protect and bless the person reading this message.' God smiled and answered . . . 'Request granted'.

"Winners are losers who got up and gave it one more try". Dennis DeYoung

"There is no scarcity of opportunity to make a living at what you love; there's only a scarcity of resolve to make it happen". Wayne Dyer

"Ability may get you to the top, but it takes character to keep you there". John Wooden

- "The soul attracts that which it secretly harbors; that which it loves, and also that which it fears". James Allen

- A Birth Certificate shows that we were born.
  A Death Certificate shows that we died.
  Pictures show that we lived!
  Have a seat . . . . Relax . . . And read this slowly.
  I Believe . . .

That just because two people argue, doesn't mean they don't love each other. And just because they <u>don't</u> argue, doesn't mean they <u>do</u> love each other. That we don't have to change friends if we understand that friends change. That no matter how good a friend is, they're going to hurt you every once in a while.

Advertising!

Signs, business cards, stickers, door hangers and pamphlets, some TV and radio and newspaper advertisements are the tools we have used to build our business. The big reason we like to use signs is this: Every time a person goes to the grocery store, Laundromat, to and from work, or even driving to the car wash, post office, drug store, etc. these signs are a constant reminder of Rent-A-Maid. Not just for cleaning, but repairs and security when they leave home for an extended period of time.

Our stickers were designed for use on trash cans, bulletin boards, store fronts where bank cards are displayed. They are the same size and they fit right in with the rest of the card. Almost anywhere people go: public phones, car wash, beauty shops, barber shops, service stations and convenience store, there's generally a place for a sign.

Don't get disheartened; kids and people will pull some of the signs down. Just replace them and go on to the bank and cash your checks. There's one more place to leave a few business cards, at the bank . . .

Have fun and ADVERTISE.

FRIENDSHIP!

I believe that true friendship continues to grow, even over the longest distance. Same goes for true love.

That you can do something in an instant that will give you heartache for life.

That it's taking me a long time to become the person I want to be.

That you should always leave loved ones with loving words. It may be the last time you see t hem.

That you can keep 0n going long after you think you can't.

We are responsible for what we do, no matter how we feel.

That either you control your attitude or it controls you.

Heroes are the people who do what has to be done when it needs to be done, regardless of the consequences.

FRUITS OF YOUR LABOR!

WHEREFORE BY THEIR FRUITS YE SHALL KNOW THEM. MATTHEW 7:20

SEX, ALCOHOL, DECEPTION (LYING) AND STEALING ARE FOUR BASIC CAUSES OF FAILURE.

THE DICTIONARY IS THE ONLY PLACE WHERE SUCCESS COMES BEFORE WORK.

DESIRE IS THE BEGINNING OF ALL HUMAN ACHIEVEMENT.

GIFTED PEOPLE ARE MADE NOT BORN.

BELIEVE YOU CAN, AND YOU CAN.

DARE TO AIM HIGH.

MANY FAIL TO RECOGNIZE OPPORTUNITY BECAUSE ITS FAVORITE DISGUISE IS HARD WORK.

WITH EVERY DISADVANTAGE THERE IS ALWAYS A GREATER ADVANTAGE.

ASK AND IT SHALL BE GIVEN YOU, SEEK AND YE SHALL FIND; KNOCK AND IT SHALL BE OPENED UNTO YOU.

Trust In Him

KEEPING SCORE!

Money is a lousy way of keeping score.

My best friend and I can do anything, or nothing, and have the best time.

Sometimes the people you expect to kick you when you're down. They will be the ones to help you get back up.

Sometimes when I'm angry I have the right to be angry, but that doesn't give me the right to be cruel.

It isn't always enough to be forgiven by others. Sometimes, you have to learn to forgive yourself.

No matter how bad your heart is broken the world doesn't stop for your grief.

Maturity has more to do with what types of experiences you've had, also what you've learned from them . . . . and less to do with hOW MANY BIRTHDAYS YOU'VE CELEBRATED.

"RENT-A-MAID"

(maid's contract)

I,_____ agree to the following rules and conditions, upon acceptance by **RENT-A-MAID.** To be paid on a payment rate_____% (tips not included).

I understand and agree that I will be bonded by a company bond, and in the event of conviction or forfeiture, I will be assessed the maximum penalty for such crime.

TERMINATION: I agree to give at least a four (4) day written notice upon termination of employment. **RENT-A-MAID** places a value of $25.00 on hiring and training. I agree that if **I do not** give a four (4) day written notice to quit, cost of training fee will be taken out of my last pay check.

For a period of one year **not** to; accept payment, work for, solicit similar or like business to/for/from customers of **RENT-A-MAID.**

I authorize investigation of all statements contained in applications made for employment with **RENT-A-MAID.** Further, I understand and agree that my employment is for no definite period and may, regardless of the date of payment of my wages, be terminated at any time without previous notice.

A fine of $300.00 will be assessed for cleaning customer's home without assignment by **RENT-A-MAID.**

Date_____ Signature_____

PEOPLE!

Our background and circumstances may have influenced who we are, but we are responsible for who we become.

You shouldn't be so eager to find out a secret. It could change your life forever.

Two people can look at the exact same thing and see something totally different.

Your life can be changed in a matter of hours by people who don't even know you.

Even when you think you have no more to give, if a friend cries out to you .... you will find the strength to help.

Credentials on the wall do not make you a decent human being.

That the people you care about most in life are taken from you too soon.

The happiest of people don't necessarily have the best of everything. They make the most of everything they have.

"RENT-A-MAID"

PERSONAL INFORMATION

DATE _____ SOCIAL SECURITY NUMBER _____

NAME _____   AGE _____   SEX _____
LAST   FIRST   MIDDLE

PRESENT ADDRESS _____
STREET   CITY   STATE

PERMANENT ADDRESS _____
STREET   CITY   STATE

PHONE NO. _____   OWN HOME _____   RENT _____   BOARD _____

DATE OF BIRTH _____   HEIGHT _____   WEIGHT _____   COLOR OF HAIR _____   COLOR OF EYES _____

MARRIED _____ SINGLE _____ WIDOWED _____ DIVORCED _____ SEPARATED _____

NUMBER OF CHILDREN _____   DEPENDENTS OTHER THAN WIFE OR CHILDREN _____   CITIZEN OF U.S.A.   YES ☐   NO ☐

IF RELATED TO ANYONE IN OUR EMPLOY, STATE NAME AND DEPARTMENT _____   REFERRED BY _____

FORMER EMPLOYERS (LIST BELOW LAST FOUR EMPLOYERS, STARTING WITH LAST ONE FIRST.)

DATE MONTH AND YEAR	NAME AND ADDRESS OF EMPLOYER	SALARY	POSITION	REASON FOR LEAVING
FROM				
TO				
FROM				
TO				
FROM				
TO				
FROM				
TO				

REFERENCES: GIVE BELOW THE NAMES OF THREE PERSONS NOT RELATED TO YOU, WHOM YOU HAVE KNOWN AT LEAST ONE YEAR.

	NAME	ADDRESS	PHONE NUMBER	YEARS ACQUAINTED
1				
2				
3				

PHYSICAL RECORD:

LIST ANY PHYSICAL DEFECTS _____

WERE YOU EVER INJURED? _____ GIVE DETAILS _____

HAVE YOU ANY DEFECTS IN HEARING? _____ IN VISION? _____ IN SPEECH? _____

IN CASE OF EMERGENCY NOTIFY _____
NAME   ADDRESS   PHONE NO.

This is just to advise you that your recent application for employment will be processed as quickly as possible. Public Law 91-508 requires that we advise you that a routine inquiry may be made which will provide applicable information concerning character, general reputation, personal characteristics and mode of living. Upon written request, additional information as to the nature and scope of the report, if one is made, will be provided.

DATE _____   SIGNATURE _____

Printed by "RENT-A-MAID" Publications

Written By Regina Brett, 90 years old, of The Plain Dealer, Cleveland, Ohio

"To celebrate growing older, I once wrote the 45 lessons life taught me. It is the most-requested column I've ever written.

My odometer rolled over to 90 in August, so here is the column once more:

1. Life isn't fair, but it's still good.

2. When in doubt, just take the next small step.

3. Life is too short to waste time hating anyone . . .

4. Your job won't take care of you when you are sick. Your friends and parents will. Stay in touch.

5. Pay off your credit cards every month.

6. You don't have to win every argument. Agree to disagree.

7. Cry with someone. It's more healing than crying alone.

8. It's OK to get angry with God. He can take it.

9. Save for retirement starting with your first paycheck.

'RENT-A-MAID'
Weekly Pay Summary

Report Date _____   Manager ☐

Name _____   Area Zip Code _____

Address _____   Regional Office _____

_____   Assigned _____

WORK DATE	CUSTOMER'S NAME	ZIP CODE	50% CLEANING AMOUNT	60% EXTRA WORK	ALL TIPS GAS	TOTAL AMOUNT
		TOTALS:				
		MGRS PAY:				

TOTAL: _____

LESS DEDUCTIONS: _____

NET PAY: _____

DATE: _____   SIGNATURE: _____

10. When it comes to chocolate, resistance is futile.

11. Make peace with your past so it won't screw up the present.

12. It's OK to let your children see you cry.

13. Don't compare your life to others. You have no idea what their journey is all about.

14. If a relationship has to be a secret, you shouldn't be in it.

15. Everything can change in the blink of an eye. But don't worry; God never blinks.

16. Take a deep breath. It calms the mind.

17. Get rid of anything that isn't useful, beautiful or joyful.

18. Whatever doesn't kill you, really does make you stronger.

19. It's never too late to have a happy childhood. But the second one is up to you and no one else.

FIELD MANAGEMENT
CERTIFICATE

KNOW ALL MEN
BY THESE PRESENTS, THAT _____

of Rent-A-Maid, at _____

    Has completed a Period of Indoctrination and has demonstrated All the qualities
of an Outstanding Individual in Leadership and Dedication to Perfection.
And is hereby designated a _____ *for Rent-A-Maid, Inc.*

        In Witness Whereof, the President of Rent-A-Maid, Inc. has
        hereunto set his hand and affixed the official Seal
        this, the _____ *day of* _____ *, 19* _____

            Rent-A-Maid of America, Inc.
            _____
                President

20.	When it comes to going after what you love in life, don't take no for an answer.

21.	Burn the candles, use the nice sheets, don't save it for a special occasion. Today is special.

22.	Over prepare, then go with the flow.

23.	Be eccentric now. Don't wait for old age to wear purple.

24.	The most important sex organ is the brain.

25.	No one is in charge of your happiness but you.

26.	Frame every so-called disaster with these words' In five years, will this matter?'

27.	Always choose life.

28.	Forgive everyone for everything.

29.	What other people think of you is none of your business.

30.	Time heals almost everything.

31.	However good or bad a situation is, it will change.

32.	Don't take yourself so seriously. No one else does.

33.	Believe in miracles.

AREA MANAGER TRAINING

1. Have at least 30 days with the company
2. Train new employees
3. Handle complaints
4. Learn Field Advertising
5. Know how to estimate houses
6. Make at least $600. Income in one month

ASSIGNED ZIP CODE AREAS

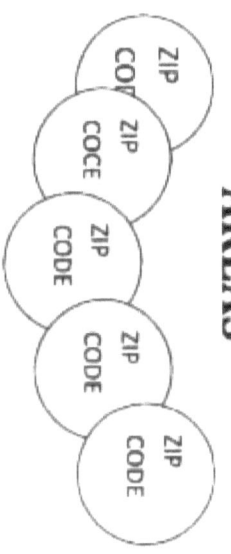

MANAGER TRAINEES MAKE 50% OF CLEANING
AREA MANAGERS MAKE 50% PLUS AREA BONUS
ON ALL WORK DONE IN THEIR ASSIGNED AREA.

'RENT-A-MAID'

AREA MANAGER

35. Don't audit life. Show up and make the most of it now.

36. Growing old beats the alternative—dying young.

37. Your children get only one childhood.

38. All that truly matters in the end is that you loved.

39. Get outside every day. Miracles are waiting everywhere.

40. If we all threw our problems in a pile and saw everyone else's, we'd grab ours back.

41. Envy is a waste of time. You already have all you need.

42. The best is yet to come.

43. No matter how you feel, get up, dress up and show up.

44. Yield.

45. Life isn't tied with a bow, but it's still a gift."

"There are four ways, and only four ways, in which we have contact with the world. We are evaluated and classified by these four contacts: what we do, how we look, what we say, and how we say it". Dale Carnegie

"The only thing that stands between a man and what he wants from life is often merely the will to try it and the faith to believe that it is possible". Richard M. DeVos

"If you're coasting, you're either losing momentum or else you're headed downhill". Joan Welsh

Thank You for your interest in Rent-A-Maid

The idea of Rent-A-Maid was created in Oklahoma City in April 1973. Four years later in July 1977, Rent-A-Maid became an Oklahoma corporation. By 1980, Rent-A-Maid was registered with the U. S. Patent and Trademark Office as a national corporation. Rent-A-Maid was approved for franchise sales by the Federal Trade Commission and the Oklahoma Securities Commission on June 1, 1994.

As an Area Manager, you will have a lot going for you. Only you will operate in a protected area under the exclusive name of Rent-A-Maid.

We will assist you throughout your operation in setting up and running your Rent-A-Maid. We will supply you with the forms, schedules, signs and business cards necessary for advertising and building your business. We also supply a "Theft Bond" for you during the first year of your operation. Most importantly, you will have a direct line to our home office to answer any questions that may arise in your everyday business operation.

We are a down-to-earth, keep it simple, type of company. Fairness and a good reputation are the most important things in building a strong business. The main focus will be banding together to learn and create a business that will grow and prosper, and one that you can be proud of.

We are looking for people who are able to step out and be independent, reaping the many benefits of owning their own businesses and working for themselves!

We are listed with the Better Business Bureau as well as Dun & Bradstreet Reporting Agency, Dallas, TX. Please check us out; we invite your response.

Our theme for the months ahead will be : "We Can Do It!" Join us and be a part of God's wonderful plan to be free to work and to live a better life than we now enjoy.

Area Managers Receive:

1. During the first 30 days of Area Manager training, you receive ___ % of cleaning amount charged plus gas allowance and tips.
2. After training, Managers receive a ___ % raise in their own production (cleaning).
3. Hourly rate for Extra Work: cleaning walls, windows, mini-blinds ovens, refrigerators or fireplaces, in addition to general cleaning is set at ___ % an hour.
4. When an area grosses ___, a bonus or rebate of ___ % will be mailed to their home by the 10th day of the following month (check in the mail).
5. Advertising in your area is very important! Rent-A-Maid will assist you in getting the best possible price on materials and supplies.
6. Checks are mailed to your home the following day after customer's checks are received by the home office for processing.
7. As an Area Manager, you will receive a beautiful certificate recognizing completion of your training period.
8. TAXES. We are not responsible, nor can we advise on filing of your taxes, although we do present tax information and working for yourself during our seminar. You will need to contact your accountant regarding your personal income tax questions.
9. CONDITIONS: Area Managers must call the office each day for next day's schedule. Area Manager assignments will be cancelled if the daily call is not received for more than 5 consecutive working days or if there is not a noticeable sign of advertising in the assigned area.
10. Theft Bond. The cost of the bond is ___ and covers theft only. It does not cover breakage. One-half of the bond amount will be deducted from the first two paychecks.

"WE CAN DO IT!"

It is up to you. You could be in business within hours of starting with us. Call our home office and together we can start the ball rolling on your new business. Call now.

67

MISSED MONMENTS!

"Please understand my friend, that where you find yourself tomorrow is a function of the positive decisions and actions you take today". Akin A. Awolaja

"When you want to encourage a greater sense of responsibility in others (and yourself), emphasize the anticipation of accomplishment, not the penalties for failure". Roger Crawford

"Opportunities are like sunrises—if you wait too long, you miss them". William Arthur Ward

"Courage is fear holding on a minute longer". Thomas Fuller

Today let your heart dance. You will find no shortage of dance partners, as your feet join in. Your eyes, your smile, and every part of your body, let your heart dance all day long.

"Character cannot be developed in ease and quiet. Only through experience of trial and suffering can the soul be strengthened, vision cleared, ambition inspired, and success achieved".—Helen Keller

"The wonderful thing about the game of life is that winning and losing are only temporary . . . unless you quit". Dr. Fred Mills

"Progress always involves risks. You can't steal second base and keep your foot on first". Frederick Wilcox

To solve any problem, here are three questions to keep in mind. First, what could I do? Second, what could I read? And third, who could I ask?

"Don't wish it were easier, wish you were better". Jim Rohn

"Take advantage of every opportunity to practice your communication skills so that when important occasions arise, you will have the gift, the style, the sharpness, the clarity, and the emotions to affect other people". Jim Rohn

There are only 3 colors, 10 digits, and 7 notes; it's what we do with them that's important. Jim Rohn

ADDITIONAL PROJECTS TO FIT YOUR NEEDS!

Rent-A Maid can help you knock out those special cleaning projects around the house. Contact your local office to discuss and schedule these special services. Some of our most popular additional cleaning projects are listed below:

OVEN/GRILL CLEANING
REFRIGERATOR CLEANING
KITCHEN CABINET CLEANING
WOOD FLOOR CLEANING
TILE FLOOR CLEANING
CONCRETE FLOOR CLEANING
WALL CLEANING
CHANDELIER CLEANING
LIGHT FIXTURES
MIRRORED WALLS
GARAGE CLEANING
VACUUM MATTRESSES
VACUUM DRAPERIES
WOOD PANELING CLEANING
FURNACE FILTER CHANGING

OUR FLAG!

"An unwritten want is a wish, a dream, a never-happen. The day you put your goal in writing is the day it becomes a commitment that will change your life. Are you ready?" Tom Hopkins

"In looking for people to hire, you look for three qualities: integrity, intelligence, and energy. And if they don't have the first, the other two will kill you." Warren Buffet

"Adversity causes some men to break; others to break records." William Arthur Ward

"The greatest thing in this world is not so much where we stand as in what direction we are moving." Johann Wolfgang von Goethe

"A great leader's courage to fulfill his vision comes from passion, not position." John Maxwell

MEANING OF THE FLAG DRAPED COFFIN . . . . All Americans should be given this lesson. Those who think that America is an arrogant nation should really reconsider that thought. Our founding fathers used GOD's word and teachings to establish our Great Nation and I think it's high time Americans get re-educated about this Nation's history.

Pass it along and be proud of the country we live in and even more proud of those who serve to protect our 'GOD GIVEN' rights and freedoms. I hope you take the time to read this . . . . To understand what the flag draped coffin really means . . . Here is how to understand the flag that laid upon it and is surrendered to so many widows and widowers. Do you know that at military funerals, the 21-gun salute stands for the sum of the numbers in the year 1776?

Home Cleaning Products Too Costly?

Try these easy and natural cleaning solutions with supplies you already have in your pantry:

Mix a paste of baking soda and vinegar to remove stubborn toilet bowl rings

Rub windows with a cotton ball dipped in rubbing alcohol to remove old cleaning product residue and rinse with a mixture of two tablespoons vinegar to one quart of water.

Polish wood using one part white vinegar to three parts olive oil.

Use baking soda for scouring or to remove scuff marks from vinyl flooring.

Add a small square of aluminum foil to boiling water and baking soda and you have a great bath to remove tarnish from silver.

OUR FLAG!

Have you ever noticed the honor guard pays meticulous attention to correctly folding the United States of America Flag 13 times? You probably thought it was to symbolize the original 13 colonies, but we learn something new every day!

The 1st fold of the flag is a symbol of life.

The 2nd fold is a symbol of the belief in eternal life.

The 3rd fold is made in honor and remembrance of the veterans departing the ranks who gave a portion of their lives for the defense of the country to attain peace throughout the world.

The 4th fold represents the weaker nature, for as American citizens trusting in God, it is to Him we turn in times of peace as well as in time of war for His divine guidance.

The 5th fold is a tribute to the country, for in the words of Stephen Decatur 'Our Country, in dealing with other countries, may she always be right; but it is still our country, right or wrong.'

The 6th fold is for where people's hearts lie. It is with their heart that they pledge allegiance to the flag of the United States of America, and the Republic for which it stands, one Nation under God, indivisible, with Liberty and Justice for all.

"Rent-A-Maid" Starter Pack"

Our 'Start-up' package includes a complete list of printable items to run your business. It Includes:

General Cleaning check-lists ....50ea.

Vacant House/apt. check-lists ....50ea.

Custom Business cards, with your phone number........................ 1,000ea.

Custom signs, with your phone number, large .... 100ea.

Maid's contract's ....50ea.

Payroll forms ....50ea.

Area Manager pamphlets..50ea.

If you work for Rent-A-Maid letters..50ea.

Scheduling Cards .... 100ea.

Also included is the 'Instruction Manual' valued at $49.00 plus shipping.

Be sure to have a security 'Thief Bond' on your maids.

Rent-A-Maid Int'l will be available to answer questions about your business.

Referrals from our 'Nat'l Advertising program' and updates to your 'Instruction Manual' will be sent to you ASAP.

This is a brief description of the 'Starter Pack'.

OUR FLAG!

The 7th fold is a tribute to its Armed Forces, for it is through the Armed Forces that they protect their country and their flag against all her enemies, whether they be found within or without the boundaries of their republic.

The 8th fold is a tribute to the one who entered into the valley of the shadow of death, that we might see the light of day.

The 9th fold is a tribute to womanhood, and Mothers. For it has been through their faith, their love, loyalty and devotion that the character of the men and women who have made this country great has been molded.

The 10th fold is a tribute to the father, for he, too, has given his sons and daughters for the defense of their country since they were first born.

The 11th fold represents the lower portion of the seal of King David and King Solomon and glorifies in the Hebrews eyes, the God of Abraham, Isaac and Jacob.

The 12th fold represents an emblem of eternity and glorifies, in the Christians eyes, God the Father, the Son and Holy Spirit.

The 13th fold, or when the flag is completely folded, the stars are uppermost reminding them of their nations motto, 'In God We Trust.'

Licensing vs. Franchising

A short discussion about greatly lowering the cost of business expansion through low cost "licensing" rather than investing in the huge expense of franchising. Why consider "Licensing"?

"Licensing" is lower cost and can be done quickly. If you are thinking about expanding your operation through franchising, licensing may be an alternative because (1) it is substantially less expensive, and (2) it takes about ten to fifteen business days to complete rather than months and months of franchises. Business Goals Often Can Be Met

It is often possible to draft a license agreement that achieves the goals of the licensor and the licensee and does not violate the various franchising laws. Existing Businesses as Potential Licensees

Existing businesses often buy a license and add the product or service to that existing business: this allows the licensee to keep his "bread winner" business going while he tests the licensing operations and thus reduces the risk on acquiring the license. Avoid Complex Government Regulation. There is little or no government regulation in licensing!

The Independent Contractor Issue

The independent contractor issue is the basis of the legal relationship between the licensor and the licensee. They are bound by a contract entered into as independent contractors.

Our Flag!

After the flag is completely folded and tucked in, it takes on the appearance of a cocked hat, ever reminding us of the soldiers who served under General George Washington, and the Sailors and Marines who served under Captain John Paul Jones, who were followed by their comrades and shipmates in the Armed Forces of the United States, preserving for them the rights, privileges and freedoms they enjoy today.
There are some traditions and ways of doing
things that have deep meaning.
In the future, you'll see flags folded and now
you will know why.
Share this with the children you love and all others who love what is
referred to, the symbol of 'Liberty
and Freedom.'

MAY GOD PROTECT US ALWAYS. ONE NATION, UNDER GOD, WITH LIBERTY AND JUSTICE FOR ALL

An Overview of Licensing!

Licensing is a business structure and method of expanding the distribution of goods and services. Rather than create a franchising business structure with the substantial costs involved, and entrepreneur who wishes to expand its business may be legally able to use a licensing legal structure. As in franchising, in licensing there can be (1) and initial upfront fee, (2) continuing royalties, (3) monthly license fees during the term of the agreement, (4) exclusive territories, and (5) long or short term agreement. However, franchising and licensing come from two distinct areas of law. Franchising is based on securities law and licensing is a form of contract law. On the other hand, licensing is merely a contract between two independent contractors, and franchise registration is not required. It is as simple as that.

Burial Cloth!

Why did Jesus fold the linen burial cloth after His resurrection? I never noticed this . . . .

The Gospel of John (20:7) tells us that the napkin, which was placed over the face of Jesus, was not just thrown aside like the grave clothes.

The Bible takes an entire verse to tell us that the napkin was neatly folded, and was placed at the head of that stony coffin.

Early Sunday morning, while it was still dark, Mary Magdalene came to the tomb and found that the stone had been rolled away from the entrance.

She ran and found Simon Peter and the other disciple, the one whom Jesus loved. She said, 'They have taken the Lord's body out of the tomb, and I don't know where they have put him!'

Peter and the other disciple ran to the tomb to see. The other disciple out ran Peter and got there first. He stopped and looked in and saw the linen cloth lying there, but he didn't go in.

Then Simon Peter arrived and went inside. He also noticed the linen wrappings lying there, while the cloth that had covered Jesus' head was folded up and lying to the side.

Was that important? Absolutely!
Is it really significant? Yes!

MATTHEW 7:7

DO UNTO OTHERS AS YOU WOULD HAVE OTHERS DO UNTO YOU.

A GREAT LEADER'S COURAGE TO FULFILL HER VISION COMES FROM PASSION, NOT POSITION.

THE DIFFERENCE BETWEEN THE IMPOSSIBLE AND THE POSSIBLE LIES IN A PERSON'S DETERMINATION.

THE PERSON THAT SAYS IT CANNOT BE DONE SHOULD NOT INTERRUPT THE PERSON WHO IS DOING IT.

DISCIPLINE IS THE BRIDGE BETWEEN GOALS AND ACCOMPLISHMENTS.

LASTING HAPPINESS, FREEDOM AND PEACE OF MIND ARE ALWAYS ATTAINED BE GIVING THEM TO SOMEONE ELSE.

WHEN YOUR'RE DOWN TO NOTHING, GOD IS UP TO SOMETHING.

WORRY LOOKS AROUND, SORRY LOOKS BACK, FAITH LOOKS UP.

THE FOLDED NAPKIN!

In order to understand the significance of the folded napkin, you have to understand a little bit about Hebrew tradition of that day.

The folded napkin had to do with the Master and Servant, and every Jewish boy knew this tradition.

When the servant set the dinner table for the master, he made sure that it was exactly the way the master wanted it.

The table was furnished perfectly, and then the servant would wait, just out of sight, until the master had finished eating, and the servant would not dare touch that table, until the master was finished.

Now if the master were done eating, he would rise from the table, wipe his fingers, his mouth, and clean his beard, and would wad up that napkin and toss it onto the table.

The servant would then know to clear the table. For in those days, the wadded napkin meant, "I'm finished."

But if the master got up from the table, and folded his napkin, and laid it beside his plate, the servant would not dare touch the table, because . . . .

The folded napkin meant,
"I'm coming back!

Amen

ONE MORE THING, DON'T FORGET THE CREDIT
CARD!!!

Rent-A-Maid International

Car Washing as an Extra to Housecleaning!

Say it takes one hour to drive their car to a self service car wash. It will cost from $2 to $4 to vacuum and wash. After washing, start with the windshield and dry all windows, then dry the hood and sides and rear of car. This should take about an hour to complete. When the customer comes home, not only is their house clean but their car is shinny & clean also.

Oh yes, if they leave an extra amount of money, you can put gas in as well. Don't you think they will tell everyone at work about that little extra that "Rent-A-Maid" will do. And you have made an extra hour for your efforts.

P.S. *Now it's your turn to think of something extra we can do for the customer.*

Get Fido and Fluffy Ready for 'Rent A Maid' Service Workers:

Tell your 'service provider' the pet's name in the event that the pet should become disagreeable or disappear. Show your service provider where you keep the pet's leash and any treats as a means to lure a missing pet back home or out of hiding.
If there is an animal mess, clean it up before the service provider arrives. Animal excrement can lead to the spread of dangerous diseases if not handled properly.
If possible, relocate your pet. Put your pet in a kennel or in a clearly marked room that the service worker is not scheduled to enter.

83

**Leave a few favorite toys with your pet to keep it
from getting restless.
If you are expecting a cleaning service, be sure to mention your pet's
favorite hang-outs so special attention can be paid to removing excess pet
dander from those areas.**

BE STRONG!

We are not here to play, to dream, to drift;

We have hard work to do, and loads to lift;

Shun not the struggle, face it; it is God's gift.

BE STRONG!

Say not, "The days are evil. Who's to blame?"

And fold the hands and acquiesce—oh shame!

Stand up, speak out, and bravely, in God's name.

BE STRONG!

It matters not how deep entrenched the wrong.

How hard the battle goes, the day how long

Faint not—fight on! To-morrow comes the song.

TIME & OPPORTUNITY IS NOW!

In Conclusion

When I was a young man starting out in life, I thought, "Boy, the old folks probably have a lot of wisdom and knowledge after all the years they've lived and all they've been through." I'm past retirement age now but I don't feel like giving up and settling down to do nothing, not yet! In these pages I've tried to give you a start to more than just the "Rent-A-Maid" business.

I've learned a few things and that is, "you can lead a horse to water, but you can't make them drink". Another old saying, "Give a person a fish and they'll eat for a day, teach them to fish and they'll have food for life".

Any business you undertake is like a postage stamp, "stick to it till you get there". Knowledge and attitude will get you a long way in any business.

One good rule in life is "keep your spending below what you make." Never bet on tomorrow, chances are it will change before you get t here. Bet on yourself and you only have yourself to blame whether you make it or not.

The Bible is the number one way I get motivated every day. If you only read a couple of pages a day, it adds s up. The biggest change in my life came in 1983 on a hill in Edmond, Oklahoma. It was July 4, about dusk. I came upon a football stadium surrounded by a lot of cars.

I pulled off the highway and found a place to park on a hill overlooking the field. Phil Driskol was playing a horn and a two hundred member choir was singing.

My life had been "rough" to say the least, up to now. I was put in an orphanage in Waco, Texas at twelve years old. That's where the "rough" began!

By this time in my life I had sung in every bar and dive in Oklahoma City, and I had written over a hundred crying, lying, dying country songs. I knew I was going nowhere in my life and by myself it wasn't going to get any better. Right there in my car I lowered my head and ask Jesus to come into my heart and forgive me of all my sins.

My life didn't change all at once, but over the next few months I stopped drinking. It took more than two years to stop smoking, and a lot longer than that to erase the dirty words from my mind. The first song I wrote after that memorial night was "If Jesus Had A Guitar".

I now have five CDs and most of them are country gospel songs. I'd say my life has changed since that moment on the hill in 1983! I recall another man's life changed on a hill, I am sure you know who. HE can change your life and give you guidance and strength every day. So . . . .

In your hands you hold the tools for a successful office. There can only be one Rent-A-Maid office in your area so decide quickly if it will be YOURS!

CALL 972-240-4098

BELIEVE IN YOURSELF!

"The person we believe ourselves to be will always act in a manner consistent with our self-image". Brian Tracy

Put off for one day, and ten days will pass.

"Everyone's life is under someone's control—it might as well be under your own so that you can direct your destiny". Harry Tucker

You cannot change anything in your life with intention alone, which can become a watered-down, occasional hope that you'll get to tomorrow. Intention without action is useless.

"Be careful the environment you choose for it will shape you;

Be careful the friends you choose for you will become like them". W. Clement Stone

"You are today where your thoughts have brought you;

You will be tomorrow where your thoughts take you". James Allen

"The size of the future you actually experience will largely be determined by one factor: the people you choose to connect with. When you invite people who are truly committed to growth into every aspect of your life, your own potential for growth becomes truly unlimited". Dan Sullivan

"You can't help someone get up a hill without getting closer to the top yourself". H. Norman Schwarzkopf

"We all have our time machines. Some take us forward, they're called dreams.

Some take us back, they're called memories". Jeremy Irons "We must not allow other people's limited perceptions to define us". Virginia Satir

"You cannot teach a man anything. You can only help him discover it within himself". Galileo

JUST IMAGINE!

JUST FOR A MOMENT, IMAGINE THAT THE SUN IS GOD
WATCHING OVER US AS WE WORK AND PLAY.
CLOUDS ARE TRIALS AND TROUBLES IN OUR LIFE TO SHOW
US A DIFFERENT DIRECTION AND BLESSINGS WE MUST
TAKE EACH DAY.
WHEN THE SUN MOVES ON TO BLESS SOMEONE ELSE. HE
GIVES US THE MOON AS THE HOLY SPRIT TO WATCH OVER
US.
WITH THE STARS BEING ANGELS, OH SO MANY. THAT
SURROND US EACH NIGHT.
EVEN WHEN CLOUDS AND RAIN SEEM TO COME BETWEEN
US, GOD AND THE HOLY SPIRIT ARE ALWAYS THERE.
LET'S IMAGINE THAT THE WIND BEING THE DEVIL, AS IT
BLOWS SOMETIMES AS A TORNADO OR HURRICANE TO
WRECK HAVOC IN OUR LIVES.
NOW JESUS IS THE KEEPER OF HEAVEN, AND WE'LL
WALK AND TALK WITH HIM ALONG THE 'RIVER OF LIFE'
SOMEDAY.
JUST IMAGINE OUR PRAYERS BEING
'E-MAIL' THAT WE CAN SEND TO HEAVEN ANYTHIME WE'RE
IN NEED. THEY GO
DIRECT TO JESUS CHRIST, THAN TO
THE HOLY SPIRIT AND HIS ANGELS TO
TAKE CHARGE OF THE EVENTS THAT SUROUND US HERE
ON EARTH.
JUST IMAGINE, FAITH, HOPE, AND LOVE, BEING CANDLES
THAT LIGHT OUR WAY AS WE STEP OUT IN THIS WORLD
TODAY.
WITH GOD BEING THE SUN, THE HOLY SPIRIT BEING THE
MOON, THE STARS BEING ANGELS, AND JESUS CHRIST
BEING THE KEEPER OF HEAVEN, LIFE GOES ON.
JUST IMAGINE!

RAY KIKER, DEC. 22, 2009

This is the First Day of the Rest of my Life!

Another new day has just begun, look out the window here comes the sun, and all the life I lived before was yesterday. For the new day leaves the past behind and I can find what's really in my mind, this is the first day of the rest of my life.

Just think of all the things I've never done, it's really not too late for me to start. Just think of all the songs I've never sung that I've carried in my heart. Another new chance has come to me to be the things I really want to be. All the world is waiting there for me like an open door. I don't know if I should laugh or cry but I've found my wings now watch me fly. This is the first day of the rest of my life.

For the new day leaves the past behind and I can find what's really in my mind. This is the first day of the rest of my life.

Author unknown.

I CLIMBED UP THE MOUNTAIN WITH JESUS!

I climbed up the mountain with Jesus~ Away from my burden and care, and, oh, what joy in His presence! Heavens glories came down on me there. I listened to words of great comfort and tasted His marvelous grace: So kind was the face of the Master! So gentle His tender embrace! I thought I would stay on the mountain to enjoy these experiences new, but Jesus spoke out from His Glory, "There is work in the valley to do". "But, Lord, there is sin in the valley, there is sorrow and suffering too, O Savior, I would so much rather stay here on the mountain with you". "There is sin," He replied, smiling kindly, "There is sorrow and suffering I know, but that is the reason, my child, that I have asked you to go." "But, Lord," I said, glancing downward, "they really don't want me down there. They are finding their joy in sin's pleasures: For my fellowship, they'll not care". "I know it, my child," came His answer, "and neither do they desire me, but, loving them, I died to save them, and you must go tell them," said He. "But, Lord, it's so dark in the valley, black darkness is there night and day." "I am the light," Jesus whispered, "and I will show you the way." I then sought the path that led downward into the valley below: And, oh, the joy of this knowledge! He is with me wherever I go!

You've had a sneak peak at a few of the 84 pages of "HOW TO OPERATE A RENT-A-MAID BUSINESS". Thanks to the internet I don't have to travel great distances to show you what I have learned in 20 years of Rent-A-Maid experience. When I began my business I would add an item needed in my business each day, week or month. The real secret revealed in the book is how easy it is to expand your business. It also gives each "Maid" a feeling of belonging and a reason to go the extra mile for her and for you. Many people have no desire to be a "Maid" for life. Some people do it out of necessity, as a part time job, or for the summer. Regardless, everyone has the ability to "clean" and with the right motivation and direction they can have a happy rewarding career!

When the Maids begin their employment they are paid 50% of the cleaning fees, plus tips. As they become experienced and build their schedules, their pay increases by bonuses, overrides and awards. Some may go on to acquire their own RENT-A-MAID offices in other cities. The cost of opening an office is established by the cost of printing of signs, forms, and office supplies to run your business for at least three months. We want to see you open and running your business instead of trying to raise capital for a franchise. Of course you will pay us a small amount for the use of the NAME and the EXCLUSIVE AREA, plus a percentage to expand into other areas thru our National Advertising Programs. Any expansion of any Rent-A-Maid business benefits all of us by the good will and advertising. You have read the pages on LICENSING and how easy it is to be a part of RENT-A-MAID. Here it is in a nut shell; the total amount to start your business is $1995.00, signing the licensing agreement and installing a business phone. At that point we start your custom printing. Follow the steps in the manual and let us know your opening date. It's that easy. You will have questions and we will answer them! Imagine your first day! "RENT-A-MAID this is (your name), may I help you? Oh yes we do that"! Or, "We're interviewing at 9 or 11 am. Which is best for you? You must have a car a phone.

CALL US 972-240-4098. DO IT NOW!

"NOTES"

Your name: **date finished reading.**
Address

Make the ultimate Sacrifice! After reading this book a couple of times, give it away! Yes, send this book to the first person you think of. In the future, wouldn't it be awesome, if you received the book back with all the names and places it has been. Prove the verse: "Give and it shall be given unto you." Luke 6: 35

www.ingramcontent.com/pod-product-compliance
Lightning Source LLC
Chambersburg PA
CBHW030413290526
45785CB00004B/1985